THE WAY
OF THE
CROSS

FR. MARK TOUPS

ASCENSION

West Chester, Pennsylvania

Nihil obstat: Reverend Samuel Brice Higginbotham
           Censor librorum
           October 15, 2019

Imprimatur: +Most Reverend Shelton J. Fabre
           Bishop of Houma-Thibodaux
           October 15, 2019

Ascension
Post Office Box 1990
West Chester, PA 19380
1-800-376-0520
ascensionpress.com

Photos by: Matthew Pirrall

Printed in the United States of America
ISBN 978-1-950784-23-3

INTRODUCTION

Like many of you, I grew up with the Stations of the Cross as a regular Lenten practice. The Stations of the Cross serve as a pilgrimage of sorts: we accompany Jesus on his journey so that we are more able to experience him during the crowning moment of his life and mission.

In his discourse with the Pharisees, Jesus says: "For this reason the Father loves me, because I lay down my life, that I may take it again. *No one takes it from me,* but I lay it down *of my own accord.* I have power to lay it down, and I have power to take it again" (John 10:17-18, emphasis added). Jesus, then, freely *chose* to give his life to save us from our sins. No one forced him; he freely chose to do so for love of us.

In Matthew 26:30 we read: "And when they had sung a hymn, they went out to the Mount of Olives." What was the hymn they sang? If Jesus was praying a hymn at *this* moment of his life, we would do well to pray it with him. The Passover script of antiquity reveals that the Last Supper would have ended with Jesus praying the "Hallel Psalms," specifically Psalms 115 through 118.

Every faithful Jewish person of his time would have prayed all 150 Psalms at least once a month, so we know Jesus prayed the Psalms throughout his life—and can safely infer that he would have prayed them during his Passion. So it is especially appropriate for us to pray and meditate on the Psalms as we celebrate the Stations of the Cross.

Using the Psalms as words into his own heart, let us accompany Jesus on his way to the Cross.

Opening Prayer

LEADER: In the name of the Father, and of the Son, and of the Holy Spirit.

May our contemplation of these sacred Stations dispose us to the graces poured forth on the world from the Cross.

ALL: We cannot rely on our own strength, for we do not know how to pray as we ought. Therefore, bless us now that we might be open to receive. Bless our minds that we might meditate on these timeless mysteries. Bless our ears that we might hear your voice. Bless our lips that we might speak your praise. Bless our hearts that we might know your love.

LEADER: Give us, O Lord, an ever-watchful heart which nothing can ever lure away from you; a noble heart, which no unworthy affection can draw downwards; an upright heart, which no sin can warp; an unconquerable heart, which no tribulation can crush; a free heart, which no perverted affection can claim for its own.

ALL: Bestow on us, O Lord, understanding to know you, diligence to seek you, and wisdom to find you, a life that pleases you, and a hope that may embrace you at the last.

LEADER: May our contemplation of these sacred Stations dispose us to the graces poured forth on the world from the Cross. May we grow to be obedient without complaint, poor without regret, patient without murmur, humble without pretense, joyous without frivolity, and truthful without disguise. Be with us, Jesus, our Lord and our God, For with great humility, we seek to make pilgrimage in your footsteps. Amen.

✝ First Station
Jesus Is Condemned to Death

LEADER: We adore you, O Christ, and we bless you ...

ALL: *Because by your holy cross you have redeemed the world.*

LEADER: Pilate said to them, "Then what shall I do with Jesus who is called Christ?" They all said, "Let him be crucified." And he said, "Why, what evil has he done?" But they shouted all the more, "Let him be crucified." Then, he released for them Barabbas, and having scourged Jesus, delivered him to be crucified. —*Matthew 27:22-23, 26*

Let us contemplate Jesus standing beside Pilate. As his eyes behold the frenetic crowds that have filled the praetorium, he can also see the remnants of palm branches that still line the streets from his entrance into Jerusalem a mere five days earlier. Let us consider Jesus silently reciting the following words of Psalm 57 as he stands atop the steps of the praetorium and hears the chants of: "Crucify him! Crucify him!" *(Pause)*

> My heart is steadfast, O God,
> my heart is steadfast!

ALL: *Be merciful to me, O God,*
be merciful to me,
for in you my soul takes refuge;
in the shadow of your wings I will take refuge,
till the storms of destruction pass by.
I cry to God Most High,
to God who fulfils his purpose for me.
He will send from heaven and save me,
he will put shame to those who trample upon me.
God will send forth his mercy and his faithfulness.
—Psalm 57:7, 1-3

✝ Second Station
Jesus Carries the Cross

LEADER: We adore you, O Christ, and we bless you ...

ALL: *Because by your holy cross you have redeemed the world.*

LEADER: [The soldiers] clothed him in a purple cloak, and plaiting a crown of thorns they put it on him. And they began to salute him, "Hail, King of the Jews!" And they struck his head with a reed, and spat upon him, and they knelt down in homage to him. And when they had mocked him, they stripped him of the purple cloak, and put his own clothes on him. And they led him out to crucify him. —*Mark 15:17-20*

Let us contemplate Jesus in his prison cell. As he beholds the soldiers who kneel before him in mockery and "homage," Jesus can see the moment when these men will kneel before him in worship at the hour of their deaths. Together, let us consider Jesus silently reciting the following words of Psalm 25 as he endures the mockery of the Roman soldiers. *(Pause)*

> To you, O Lord, I lift up my soul.
> Oh my God, in you I trust,
> let me not be put to shame;
> let not my enemies exalt over me.

ALL: *My eyes are ever toward the Lord,*
for he will pluck my feet out of the net.
Turn to me, and be gracious to me;
for I am lonely and afflicted.
Relieve the troubles of my heart,
and bring me out of my distresses.
Oh, guard my life, and deliver me;
Let me not be put to shame, for I take refuge in you.
—Psalm 25:1-2, 15-17, 20

✝ Third Station
Jesus Falls the First Time

LEADER: We adore you, O Christ, and we bless you ...

ALL: *Because by your holy cross you have redeemed the world.*

LEADER: Surely, he has borne our griefs, and carried our sorrows. But he was wounded for our transgressions, he was bruised for our iniquities. Upon him was the chastisement that made us whole, and with his stripes we were healed.
—*Isaiah 53:4, 5*

Let us contemplate Jesus as he falls under the weight of the Cross. The merciless scourging from the Roman soldiers has left him weakened. The wounds on his back add to Jesus' struggle to bear his cross, and with each stride he is pierced with the pain of this journey. As he collapses to the ground, all Jesus can see are the feet of those who swarm around him in ridicule. As Jesus hears their jeers and slander, let us together consider him silently reciting the following words of Psalm 35. *(Pause)*

> But at my stumbling they gathered in glee,
> they gathered together against me;
> cripples whom I did not know
> slandered me without ceasing;
> they impiously mocked more and more,
> gnashing at me with their teeth.

ALL: *You have seen, O LORD; be not silent!*
O Lord be not far from me!
Vindicate me, O LORD, my God,
according to your righteousness;
and let them not rejoice over me!
—*Psalm 35:15-16, 22, 24*

✝ **Fourth Station**
Jesus Meets His Mother

LEADER: We adore you, O Christ, and we bless you ...

ALL: Because by your holy cross you have redeemed the world.

LEADER: Simeon blessed them and said to Mary his mother, "Behold, this child is set for the fall and rising of many in Israel, and for a sign that is spoken against (and a sword will pierce through your own soul also) that thoughts out of many hearts may be revealed." And his mother kept all these things in her heart. —*Luke 2:34-35, 51*

Let us contemplate Jesus as he meets his mother on the Way of the Cross. The Psalms were at the heart of Jewish spirituality and therein would have been at the heart of life for the Holy Family in Nazareth. Mary and Jesus would have chanted the Psalms daily. Let us consider Jesus' eyes meeting his mother's eyes. Then, just as they would have done in Nazareth, let us imagine Jesus intoning the opening verse and then the two of them together reciting the remainder of Psalm 31. *(Pause)*

> In you, O LORD, I seek refuge;
> let me never be put to shame;
> in your righteousness deliver me!
> Incline your ear to me,
> rescue me speedily!
> Be a rock of refuge for me,
> a strong fortress to save me!

ALL: Be strong, and let your heart take courage,
All you who wait for the LORD!
   —*Psalm 31:1-2, 24*

✝ Fifth Station
Simon Helps Jesus Carry the Cross

LEADER: We adore you, O Christ, and we bless you ...

ALL: Because by your holy cross you have redeemed the world.

LEADER: As they were marching out, they came upon a man of Cyrene, Simon by name; this man they compelled to carry his cross. —*Matthew 27:32*

LEADER: Let us consider Jesus looking deep into the eyes of Simon the Cyrenian. Simon's arms meet the arms of Jesus, wrapped around the Cross. Simon can feel the exhaustion of Jesus' body begging for help. As their eyes meet, and their arms intertwine, Jesus whispers the words of Psalm 69 to Simon. *(Pause)*

> Let not those who hope in you be put to
> shame through me
> O LORD God of hosts;
> let not those who seek you be brought to
> dishonor through me,
> O God of Israel.
> For zeal for your house has consumed me,
> and the insults of those who insult you have
> fallen on me.

*ALL: But as for me, my prayer is to you, O LORD.
At an acceptable time, O God,
in the abundance of your mercy, answer me.
But I am afflicted and in pain;
let your salvation, O God, set me on high!
I will praise the name of God with a song;
I will magnify him with thanksgiving.
—Psalm 69:6, 9, 13, 29-30*

✝ Sixth Station
Veronica Wipes the Face of Jesus

LEADER: We adore you, O Christ, and we bless you …

ALL: *Because by your holy cross you have redeemed the world.*

LEADER: He had no form or comeliness that we should look at him, and no beauty that we should desire him. He was despised and rejected by men; a man of sorrows, and acquainted with grief; and as one from whom men hide their faces he was despised, and we esteemed him not.
—*Isaiah 53:2-3*

Let us contemplate Veronica wiping the face of Jesus. As she tenderly wipes away the blood from his face, Jesus' eyes shine bright beneath the removed blood. Together, let us consider Jesus looking deep into Veronica's eyes and offering the words of Psalm 20 in gratitude. *(Pause)*

> The LORD answer you in the day of trouble!
> The name of the God of Jacob protect you!
> May he send you help from the sanctuary,
> And give you support from Zion!
> May he remember all your offerings,
> and regard with favor your burnt sacrifices!
> May he grant you your heart's desire, and fulfill all
> your plans!

ALL: *Now I know the LORD will help his anointed;*
he will answer him from his holy heaven
with mighty victories by his right hand.
Give victory to the king, O LORD;
answer us when we call!
—Psalm 20:1-4, 6, 9

✝ **Seventh Station**
Jesus Falls the Second Time

LEADER: We adore you, O Christ, and we bless you ...

ALL: *Because by your holy cross you have redeemed the world.*

LEADER: Be gracious to me, O Lᴏʀᴅ, for I am in distress; my eye is wasted from grief, my soul and body also. For my life is spent with sorrow, and my years with sighing; my strength fails because of my misery, and my bones waste away.
—*Psalm 31:9-10*

Let us contemplate Jesus as he lies face down on the ground under the weight of the Cross and silently recites the following words of Psalm 56. *(Pause)*

> Have mercy on me, O God, for men trample upon me;
> all day long foes oppress me;
> my enemies trample upon me all day long;
> for many fight against me proudly.
> When I am afraid,
> I put my trust in you.

ALL: *In God, whose word I praise,*
in God I trust without a fear.
For you have delivered my soul from death,
yes, my feet from falling,
that I may walk before God
in the light of life.
> —*Psalm 56:1-3, 10-11, 13*

✝ Eighth Station
Jesus Meets the Women of Jerusalem

LEADER: We adore you, O Christ, and we bless you ...

ALL: Because by your holy cross you have redeemed the world.

LEADER: But Jesus turning to them said, "Daughters of Jerusalem, do not weep for me; but weep for yourselves and for your children. For behold, the days are coming when they will say, 'Blessed are the barren, the wombs that never bore and the breasts that never nursed!' Then they will begin to say to the mountains, 'Fall on us'; and to the hills, 'Cover us.' For if they do this when the wood is green, what will happen when it is dry?" —*Luke 23:28-31*

Let us contemplate Jesus remembering the words of Psalm 34 as he meets the women of Jerusalem. *(Pause)*

> The eyes of the LORD are toward the righteous,
> and his ears toward their cry.
> When the righteous cry for help, the LORD hears,
> and delivers them out of all their troubles.
> The LORD is near to the brokenhearted, and saves the crushed in spirit.

ALL: Many are the afflictions of the righteous;
but the LORD delivers him out of them all.
He keeps all his bones;
not one of them is broken.
The LORD redeems the life of his servant,
None of those who take refuge in him will be condemned.
—Psalm 34:15, 17-18, 19-20, 22

✝ **Ninth Station**
Jesus Falls a Third Time

LEADER: We adore you, O Christ, and we bless you ...

ALL: Because by your holy cross you have redeemed the world.

LEADER: He was oppressed, and he was afflicted, yet he opened not his mouth; when he makes himself an offering for sin, he shall see his offspring, he shall prolong his days, the will of the LORD shall prosper in his hand; he shall see the fruit of the travail of his soul and be satisfied; by his knowledge shall the righteous one, my servant, make many to be accounted righteous; and he shall bear their iniquities.
—*Isaiah 53:7, 10-11*

Let us contemplate Jesus as he falls a third time. Even with Simon's assistance, the abuse during his arrest in the Garden, the exhaustion from being imprisoned, and the torture of the scourging have all taken a toll on his body. In that moment, Jesus could have clung to the words of Psalm 41. *(Pause)*

> My enemies say of me in malice:
> 'When will he die, and his name perish?'
> And when one comes to see me,
> he utters empty words.

ALL: But you, O LORD, be gracious to me,
and raise me up, that I may repay them!
By this I know that you are pleased with me,
in that my enemy has not triumphed over me.
But you have upheld me because of my integrity,
and set me in your presence forever.
Blessed be the LORD, the God of Israel,
from everlasting to everlasting!
*   —Psalm 41:5-6, 10-13*

✝ **Tenth Station**
Jesus Is Stripped of His Garments

LEADER: We adore you, O Christ, and we bless you ...

ALL: *Because by your holy cross you have redeemed the world.*

LEADER: When the soldiers had crucified Jesus, they took his garments and made four parts, one for each soldier; also, his tunic. But the tunic was without seam, woven from top to bottom; so they said to one another, "Let us not tear it, but cast lots for it to see whose it shall be." —*John 19:23*

Let us contemplate Jesus praying Psalm 22 as he is stripped of his garments. *(Pause)*

> All who see me mock at me,
> they make mouths at me,
> they wag their heads;
> "He committed his cause to the LORD;
> let him deliver him,
> let him rescue him, for he delights in him!"

ALL: *Be not far from me,*
for trouble is near,
and there is none to help.
I can count all my bones--
they stare and gloat over me;
they divide my garments among them,
and for my clothing they cast lots.
But you, O LORD, be not far off!
O my help, hasten to my aid!
—Psalm 22:7-8, 11, 17-19

✝ **Eleventh Station**
Jesus Is Nailed to the Cross

LEADER: We adore you, O Christ, and we bless you …

ALL: *Because by your holy cross you have redeemed the world.*

LEADER: And when they came to the place which is called the Skull, there they crucified him, and the criminals, one on the right and one on the left. —*Luke 23:33*

Let us contemplate Jesus praying Psalm 116 as he is nailed to the Cross, recalling how these were the very words Jesus prayed as he left the Last Supper. *(Pause)*

> I love the LORD, because he has heard
> my voice and my supplications.
> Because he inclined his ear to me,
> Therefore, I will call on him as long as I live.
> The snares of death encompassed me;
> the pangs of Sheol laid hold on me;
> I suffered distress and anguish.
> Then I called on the name of the LORD:
> "O LORD, I beg you, save my life!"

ALL: *What shall I render to the LORD*
for all his bounty to me?
I will lift up the chalice of salvation
and call on the name of the LORD,
Precious in the sight of the LORD
is the death of his saints.
   —*Psalm 116:1-4, 12-13, 15*

✝ Twelfth Station
Jesus Dies on the Cross

LEADER: We adore you, O Christ, and we bless you …

ALL: Because by your holy cross you have redeemed the world.

LEADER: After this Jesus, knowing that all was now finished, said (to fulfil the Scripture), "I thirst." A bowl of vinegar stood there; so, they put a sponge full of the vinegar on hyssop and held it to his mouth. When Jesus had received the vinegar, he said, "It is finished"; and he bowed his head and gave up his spirit. —*John 19:28-30*

Pause for extended meditation

Let us contemplate Jesus praying Psalm 118 as he hangs upon the Cross, recalling how these were the very words he prayed as he left the Last Supper. *(Pause)*

> Give thanks to the Lord, for he is good,
> his mercy endures forever.
> Out of my distress I called on the Lord;
> the Lord answered me and set me free.
> With the Lord on my side I do not fear.
> What can man do to me?

ALL: I shall not die, but I shall live,
and recount the deeds of the Lord.
I thank you that you have answered me
and have become my salvation.
O give thanks to the Lord, for he is good;
For his mercy endures forever.
—Psalm 118:1, 5-6, 17, 21, 29

✝ **Thirteenth Station**

The Body of Jesus Is Taken Down from the Cross

LEADER: We adore you, O Christ, and we bless you ....

ALL: Because by your holy cross you have redeemed the world.

LEADER: Since it was the day of preparation, in order to prevent the bodies from remaining on the cross on the sabbath (for that sabbath day was a high day), the Jews asked Pilate that their legs might be broken, and that they might be taken away. So, the soldiers came and broke the legs of the first, and of the other who had been crucified with him; but when they came to Jesus and saw that he was already dead, they did not break his legs. But one of the soldiers pierced his side with a spear, and at once there came out blood and water. For these things took place that the Scripture might be fulfilled, "Not a bone of him shall be broken." —*John 19:31-34, 36*

When Jesus was an infant, Mary would have held him close and rocked him to sleep. Let us contemplate Mary praying Psalm 55 as she rocks back and forth, holding the body of her Son in her arms. *(Pause)*

> Give ear to my prayer, O God;
> and hide not yourself from my supplication!
> My heart is in anguish within me,
> the terrors of death have fallen upon me.

*ALL: But I will call upon God,
and the Lord will save me.
He will deliver my soul in safety
from the battle that I wage,
for many are arrayed against me.
But I will trust in you.*
    —*Psalm 55:1, 4, 16, 18, 23*

✝ Fourteenth Station
Jesus Is Laid in the Tomb

LEADER: We adore you, O Christ, and we bless you …

ALL: Because by your holy cross you have redeemed the world.

LEADER: And Joseph took the body, and wrapped it in a clean linen shroud, and laid it in his own new tomb, which he had hewn in the rock; and he rolled a great stone to the door of the tomb and departed. —*Matthew 27:59-60*

When Jesus was a child, Mary would have placed Jesus in his bed when he had fallen asleep. Let us contemplate Mary praying Psalm 119 as she places the body of her Son in the tomb. *(Pause)*

> My soul melts away for sorrow;
> strengthen me according to your word!
> I have chosen the way of faithfulness,
> I set your ordinances before me.
> I cling to your testimonies, O Lord;
> let me not be put to shame.

ALL: This is my comfort in my affliction,
that your promise gives me life.
Godless men utterly deride me,
but I do not turn away from your law.
Let your hand be ready to help me,
for I have chosen your precepts.
I long for your salvation, O Lord,
and your law is my delight.
—Psalm 119:28, 30-31, 50-51, 173-174

Concluding Prayer
Prayer of Saint Thomas Aquinas

LEADER: O merciful God, grant that I may ever perfectly do your will in all things. Let it be my ambition to work only for your honor and glory.

ALL: Let me rejoice in nothing but what leads to you, nor grieve for anything that leads away from you.

LEADER: May all passing things be as nothing in my eyes, and may all that is yours be dear to me, and you, my God, dear above them all.

ALL: May all joy be meaningless without you and may I desire nothing apart from you. May all labor and toil delight me when it is for you.

LEADER: Make me, O Lord, obedient without complaint, poor without regret, patient without murmur, humble without pretense, joyous without frivolity, and truthful without disguise.

ALL: Give me, O God, an ever-watchful heart which nothing can ever lure away from you; a noble heart, which no unworthy affection can draw downwards to the earth; an upright heart, which no evil can warp; an unconquerable heart, which no tribulation can crush; a free heart, which no perverted affection can claim for its own. Bestow on me, O God, understanding to know you, diligence to seek you, and wisdom to find you; a life which may please you, and a hope which may embrace you at the last.

LEADER: In the name of the Father, and of the Son, and of the Holy Spirit. Amen.

THE STABAT MATER

THE FIRST STATION
Is there one who would not weep,
whelmed in miseries so deep,
Christ's dear Mother to behold?

THE SECOND STATION
Can the human heart refrain
from partaking in her pain,
in that Mother's pain untold?

THE THIRD STATION
For his people's sins rejected,
Saw her Jesus unprotected.
Saw with thorns, with scourges rent.

THE FOURTH STATION
O how sad and sore distressed
Was that Mother, highly blessed,
Of the Sole-Begotten One.

THE FIFTH STATION
O, thou Mother, fount of love!
Touch my spirit from above,
make my heart with thine accord.

THE SIXTH STATION
Make me feel as thou hast felt;
make my soul to glow and melt
with the love of Christ my Lord.

THE SEVENTH STATION
Holy Mother! pierce me through,
in my heart each wound renew
of my Savior crucified.

THE EIGHTH STATION
Let me share with thee his pain,
who for all my sins was slain,
who for me in torments died.

THE NINTH STATION
Let me mingle tears with thee,
mourning him who mourned for me,
all the days that I may live.

THE TENTH STATION
By the Cross with thee to stay,
there with thee to weep and pray,
is all I ask of thee to give.

THE ELEVENTH STATION
Virgin of all virgins blest!
Listen to my fond request:
let me share thy grief divine.

THE TWELFTH STATION
Christ above in torment hangs,
she beneath beholds the pangs
of her dying glorious Son.

THE THIRTEENTH STATION
Through her heart, his sorrow sharing,
all his bitter anguish bearing,
now at length, the sword has passed.

THE FOURTEENTH STATION
At the cross her station keeping
Stood the mournful Mother weeping
Close to Jesus to the last.